This book is my personal record of healing;
if found, please return to:

BY THE SAME AUTHOR

RETURN TO CENTER

The Flowering of Self-Trust

ISBN: 0-87516-554-0

Healing Now

Healing Now

A PERSONAL GUIDE THROUGH CHALLENGING TIMES

Photography and Text

by

Bobbie Probstein

NORTH STAR PUBLICATIONS

GEORGETOWN, MASSACHUSETTS

International Standard Book Number: 1-880823-00-4

First Edition, 1991

NOTE: This publication and its contents are intended for educational use only and are not intended as a substitute for supervised professional, medical, psychiatric or psychological counseling or treatment. The publisher disclaims liability for any use of this publication other than the intended use expressed above.

Published by
NORTH STAR PUBLICATIONS, INC.
P.O. BOX 10
GEORGETOWN, MASSACHUSETTS 01833

Printed in the United States of America

For Larry.......the love of my life,
whose help and humor sweeten each day.

Acknowledgments

My loving thanks to my dear family: Larry, Linde, Dan and Mookie, Denny and Michael, and to the Inside Edge, my extended family of choice…all creative people.

I appreciate the support of Sanford Drucker, Leon Gottlieb, Jane Schoenberg and Ruth Avergon, and offer special thanks to Judi Donin and Dale West for their expert help. My enduring gratitude goes to George Trim for making the production and publication of **Healing Now** an experience of joy and inspiration.

Nearly twenty-five hundred years ago,
Hippocrates, (the 'father' of medicine),
said these profound words:

"A wise person should consider that
health is the greatest of human blessings,
and learn how, by his own thought, to
derive benefit from his illnesses."

I wrote this book and illustrated it with some of my favorite photographs because I know personally that these healing suggestions and images really do work. They helped me even when I didn't believe them wholeheartedly. I learned through my own experience that changing my thoughts and attitude helped me to heal.

Put this book to work for you…if you want to.
You **always** have choices.

Bobbie Probstein

This book offers suggestions that may ease difficult days. It reminds us that when we are open to healing, it comes from within and without…..and in many forms.

Open

When we learn to use our own healing potential to supplement the vast resources of medicine, we forge a powerful team to create improved health.

You can take important steps to promote healing by becoming aware of your deepest feelings and thoughts. You can change negative ideas into positive statements. This book will show you how to do it.

Which do you believe helps you more: "I am a victim. I am powerless." Or: **I HAVE THE POWER TO HEAL**!

You **always** have the choice to be negative or positive. Negative thoughts do not promote healing. Positive thoughts do.

Change

Discover

You have everything to gain
and nothing to lose
when you practice positive thinking.
You **CAN** change how you feel.

When you take responsibility
for your thoughts and feelings,
you **CAN** improve your life.

You are like an explorer
discovering a peaceful harbor.

Choose

You begin by becoming aware of what you think. Gloomy thoughts darken your days; positive thoughts make you feel brighter. Follow a dark thought with one that is positive. Only you can choose.

Thoughts are choices. Our thoughts are powerful, and evoke body responses even if we don't feel them. Positive thoughts often seem to help the immune system.

Use every resource to help healing. Repeat:
I ENJOY THINKING POSITIVE THOUGHTS!

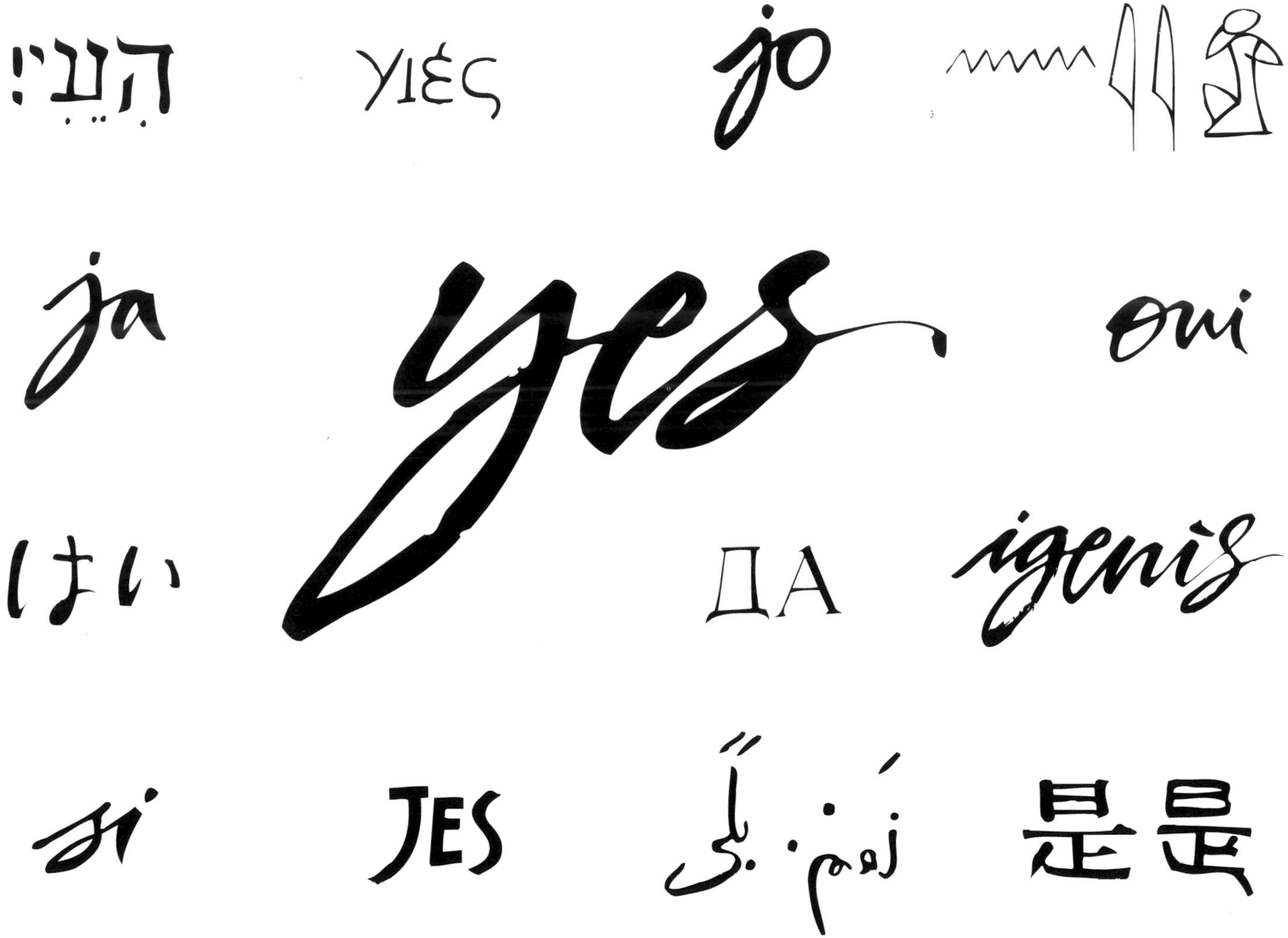
jo
ja
yes
oui
はい
ДА
igenis
si
JES
بلى
نعم
是是

I AM TAKING
AN ACTIVE PART IN
MY HEALING!

Every life may be improved in some way.

Specify what you want when you ask for it.
If you plant onions, you get onions.
If you plant flowers, you get flowers.
Plant positive thoughts.

Help your recovery.
Let your healing thoughts grow like a garden.

SPECIFY

Allow yourself to relax completely.

First, get as comfortable as you can. Loosen your clothing. Breathe slowly and deeply. Notice how the breath moves in and out of your body like the tide. Feel yourself quieting. Take as much time as you need.

Imagine you're in a place where healing happens naturally. See yourself as healthy, enjoying a wonderful vacation. Hear it, smell it, taste it, touch it…the more real the images become, the more powerful the message. You're the star, writer and director of your own movie.

Imagine

Visualize

Sometimes healing can be a slow process.
Worry and fear may creep in.

Do you know what worry is? It's imagining
what you **don't** want to happen really happening.

Instead, visualize yourself getting better. Put
positive images in your mind, instead of what
you fear. Persistence pays off…in the long run.

Think: **I AM HEALING NOW**!

Listen

Where is the peace in your life?

It is time to find it. By whatever means you choose, seek peace and make peace with yourself and those around you. There is no greater gift you can give or receive. When you accept yourself as you are, you find an island of tranquility.

If prayer and meditation are appropriate for you, make time each day to listen to your own inner voice and the profound wisdom that is our heritage from the world's religions.

To every thing there is a season, and a time
to every purpose under the heaven.
A time to be born, and a time to die; a time to plant,
and a time to pluck up that which is planted;
A time to kill, and a time to heal; a time to
break down, and a time to build up;
A time to cast away stones, and a time to
gather stones together; a time to embrace,
and a time to refrain from embracing;
A time to get, and a time to lose; a time to
keep, and a time to cast away;
A time to rend, and a time to sew; a time to
keep silence, and a time to speak;
A time of love, and a time of hate; a time of
war, and a time of peace.

The Bible, New King James Version
Old Testament, Ecclesiastes 3: 1-8

If you're in pain, it is hard to think of anything else.

But pain can be a great teacher, because it changes your priorities…if you're willing to listen. Pain teaches you to appreciate your life more, even though you may not recognize the message at the time.

Accept that you are doing the very best you can under the circumstances!

Accept

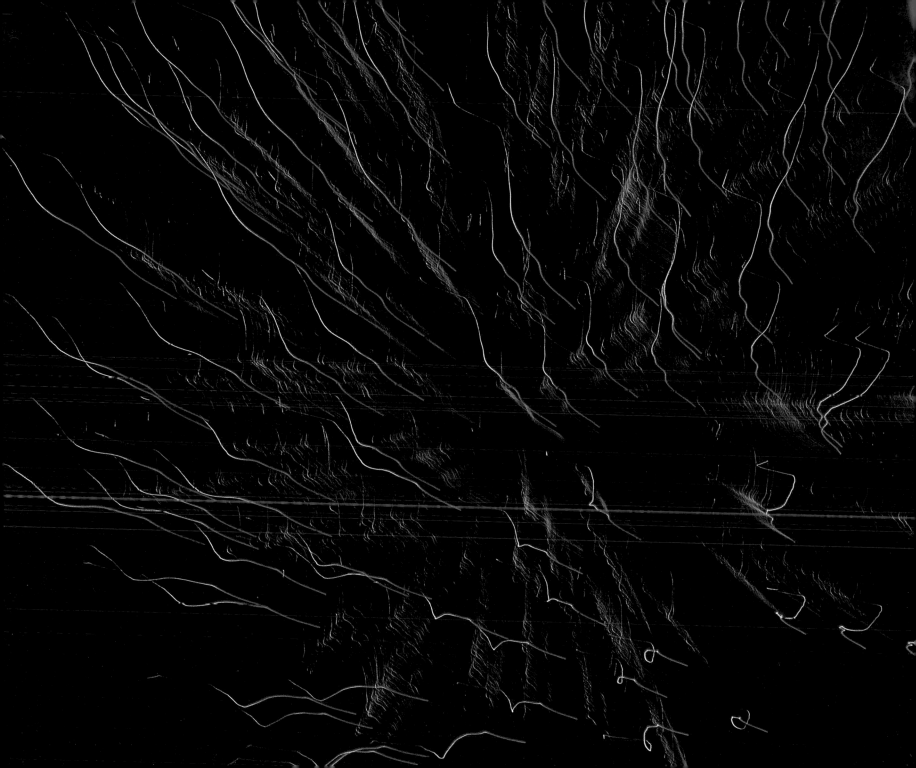

Forgive

Sometimes forgiveness
is as healing as raindrops.

Forgiving yourself for not feeling well
is a healthy practice.

Healing takes place on many levels…
physical, emotional and spiritual.

Think: **EACH DAY I CREATE MY LIFE AGAIN
BY EVERYTHING I THINK AND DO**!

Your partnership with your medical team
is a balancing force in your life.

Physicians, hospitals, and health care workers
bring knowledge, experience, and dedication to
your well being. But it is **your** body, **your**
health, **your** attitude, and **your** life.

When you affirm improved health as your goal,
you form a partnership with your doctor.
You take responsibility for your life.
You become a team with a winning goal:
YOUR GOOD HEALTH.

Tell your doctors that you appreciate their help and want to actively share in your own recovery. Should you require surgery or treatments, ask your medical team to repeat reassuring positive suggestions…even if you feel awkward requesting it at first.

Your inner mind will hear everything, although sedation may blur awareness. Positive statements work very well when your inner mind has no interference from the conscious mind.

Give each of your health professionals a copy of the healing suggestions. Ask the anesthesiologist to please repeat them as often as possible and add additional positive statements. Make sure you discuss this **BEFORE** the procedures!

ASK

heal

It is becoming widely accepted among physicians and health care staff that positive statements can be very helpful during surgery and recovery.

Have the surgical team repeat these statements often to you, plus any others they think are helpful:

✔ YOU WILL GIVE US A CLEAR FIELD!

✔ YOU ARE ALLOWING PERFECT SURGERY!

✔ YOU'RE DOING FINE! KEEP UP THE GOOD WORK!

✔ YOUR HEALING WILL BEGIN IMMEDIATELY!

✔ YOU HAVE THE ABILITY TO HEAL!

You need a peaceful setting for your recovery.
You need time to heal.

Encourage positive attitudes from friends and family.
They want to help, but may not know how.

Ask others to shop, prepare a meal, do errands, and
help with some of your responsibilities until you're able
to handle them again. When you ask for help in specific
ways, you enable others to take part in your healing process.
You benefit the giver and the receiver.

Express your gratitude and appreciation openly to all who help your healing. When you thank others as you would wish to be thanked, you fill each day with beauty.

Appreciate

As you recover, it is important to repeat
the following assertions and any others you
feel are especially helpful:

I HAVE THE POWER TO HEAL!

I ENJOY THINKING POSITIVE THOUGHTS!

I AM HEALING NOW!

I VALUE MYSELF NO MATTER WHAT IS
HAPPENING IN MY LIFE!

EACH DAY I CREATE MY LIFE AGAIN BY
EVERYTHING I THINK AND DO!

Many patients enjoy and benefit from making their own signs to remind themselves that healing is a continual process. Four of the very best words you can use are:

I am healing now!

Make the reminders big and small. Put them on your mirror, next to your bed, in the kitchen, on the walls. You're the artist! Say the words with feeling; let them echo in your body.

Many have found it helpful to log their healing journeys by keeping notes.

IT IS HARD TO KNOW HOW FAR YOU'VE COME UNTIL YOU REMEMBER WHERE YOU STARTED.

Making notes of your experiences, feelings and observations is useful for this journey. You may find new places of peace and understanding in your life.

Your personal notes do not have to be well written or correctly spelled; they only have to tell the truth as you experience it!

You have the opportunity to

Record

your feelings!

Notes - Feelings - Observations

I am healing now!

Notes - Feelings - Observations

I am healing now!

Notes - Feelings - Observations

I am healing now!

Notes - Feelings - Observations

I am healing now!

As your healing continues, remember to acknowledge what you have accomplished. It is time to cherish yourself for all the excellent work you've done and will continue to do.

Acknowledge yourself!

These two pages are for the signatures and comments of those who have helped in your recovery. You might want to say, "You have been an important part of my healing," and ask them to sign your copy of

Healing Now

In addition to your medical team, nurses and other health professionals, family and friends will appreciate being recognized as supportive and helpful.

Please sign my copy of *Healing Now*

You have made an important contribution to my healing.

I hope you continue to use and enjoy this book. Just glancing at the pictures or remembering a key word may bring back what you have read.

Best Wishes!

Bobbie

Photography
Notes and Locations

"Change"   Rhodes, Greece
"Discover"   Cayman Island, Caribbean Sea
"Imagine"   Laguna Beach, California
"Listen"   Rum Point, Caribbean Sea
"Recover"   Lake Como, Italy
"Record"   Dana Point, California

Most of the flower photographs were shot at
Butchart Gardens, Victoria, British Columbia, Canada.

This book is designed so that the photographs may
be removed and placed in a standard 8" x 10" frame.

HEALING SUGGESTIONS

- ✔ YOU WILL GIVE US A CLEAR FIELD!

- ✔ YOU ARE ALLOWING PERFECT SURGERY!

- ✔ YOU'RE DOING FINE! KEEP UP THE GOOD WORK!

- ✔ YOUR HEALING WILL BEGIN IMMEDIATELY!

- ✔ YOU HAVE THE ABILITY TO HEAL!